Talk Ain't Cheap...It's *Priceless!*

Connecting in a Disconnected World

Eileen McDargh

WALKTHETALK.COM

Resources for Personal and Professional Success

Helping Individuals and Organizations Achieve Success
Through Values-Based Practices.

Talk Ain't Cheap...It's *Priceless!*

Printed in the United States of America
10 9 8 7 6 5 4 3 2

Edited by Michelle Sedas
Cover Design by Stephen Wulf
Printed by Branch-Smith

ISBN 1-885228-85-6

Introduction

If you look closely at great places to work and companies with high levels of worker engagement and retention, you'll find a common factor. At the core, hidden behind policies and procedures, is a simple human ingredient: connected people.

Somewhere along the line, team members talk to each other to understand mutual goals. Leaders express gratitude and create a place where people feel valued. Somewhere along the line, leaders step from behind desks to listen to what people need, to ask deep questions, to seek critical feedback, and to share information that gives the WHY behind the WHAT.

Look at the underlined words. Every one of these words makes up the most critical connector of all: conversation. In great places to work, the phrase "Stop talking and get to work" has been replaced with "Start talking and get to work." Why? Because failure to use the full range of human communication skills causes a nosedive in productivity, profit, performance, and personal commitment.

You've seen what happens when communication fails and conversation is shortchanged by a one-dimensional e-mail blast or a ponderous PowerPoint presentation. At some time in your career, you've shaken your head and said, "Nobody communicates around here!" The results of living under the dictate to "Stop talking and get to work" can have severe consequences.

When Communication Fails:

- Unclear instructions cause tasks to be repeated.

- Employees kept in the dark create rumors, causing morale and performance to plummet.

- Insensitive and inappropriate communication creates tension and ill will.

- Precious time is wasted in meetings that are data dumps rather than opportunities for candid dialogue and meaningful results.

- Valuable employees feel ignored, so they leave—either physically or mentally.

- Interpersonal conflict—most always the result of poor communication—creates a stressful environment and an increase in absenteeism, health claims, and performance problems.

- Disconnected employees provide slipshod customer service.

- Disconnected customers look for a competitor who will actually talk to them and solve their problems.

For all these reasons and more, being able to connect with the hearts and minds of customers, colleagues, and employees has never been more important. Without connection, customers don't give us their time and employees don't give us their talent. You know, at an intuitive level, that talk is not cheap. It IS priceless.

Here's the challenge. As priceless as it is, communication is one of the most difficult leadership skills to master. It's easier to draft a spreadsheet, to analyze outflow, to diagram an organizational chart, or to perform any myriad of "tasks" than it is to learn how to deal with the softest part of business, the human element.

That's why a Towers Perrin global web survey of 86,000 people reported that only 14% of employees said they were highly engaged in their work. The majority expressed skepticism about leadership, especially in terms of management's vision, ability to inspire, commitment to communication, and interest in employee well-being.

You're holding in your hand a resource to help break those dismal statistics. People don't plan to be careless communicators, lousy listeners, or terrible talkers. We just take verbal communication for granted. We're often unaware of what we say and do, which can keep people from working with us and for us.

This small book offers concrete advice, action steps, and insights to help sharpen this critical leadership skill. You'll start with a personal inventory to raise awareness and then you will find simple ideas and strategies that you can put into action with your team.

Like other leaders who discover the simple power of connecting, you'll generate great results. Firms with effective communication, when compared to competitors with poor communication:

- Have a 19.4% higher stock price.

- Have a 57% higher shareholder return.

- Are 4.5 times as likely to report a high level of employee engagement.

- Are 20% more likely to have low turnover rates.*

The data proves it: In business, the intangibles drive the tangibles. How people feel at the end of a day influences their performance tomorrow.

* Watson Wyatt study of 335 public North American Companies.

If you choose to put these ideas into play, not only will you find yourself creating better results, but you will put yourself on a fast track for more leadership roles. When selecting employees for leadership positions at all levels, the management skill that organizations desire most in their future leaders is the power to motivate and engage others through their ability to communicate effectively, strategically, and interpersonally.

If you yearn to be a *great leader,*

then you must learn to be a

superb communicator.

For your success, talk ain't cheap.

It's priceless.

Table of Contents

"Only Connect!"

—E. M. Forster, *Howard's End*

Priceless Talk:

Where do you start?

We have plenty of excuses as to WHY we don't talk. The world doesn' look like the "good ol' days." In today's world, we must deal with a global econ omy, virtual teams, communication technology and the common belief that we have "Too much to do and too little time."

> *"Toto,*
>
> *I don't think*
>
> *we're in Kansas*
>
> *anymore."*
>
> —Dorothy

GLOBAL ECONOMY

Kansas. Kuwait. Killarney. Maybe even Asteroid K-66. Who knows where this 24/7 global eco nomic spaceship will carry us! Leaders at all levels of an organization might very well find themselves responding at unusual times to colleagues, ven dors, and customers. We make it brief—to honor the time zones. Talk seems a luxury—or so we think. Starbucks founder Howard Schultz would get up at 5:00 a.m. daily to TALK to general managers around the globe—to have personal conversations, check on challenges, and congratu late on effort. A luxury?

VIRTUAL TEAMS

Virtual teams float in a technology soup that has them wired with data and facts but rarely connected as individuals with minds and hearts and homes. I've witnessed team members who suddenly realize they know nothing about each other besides their "name, rank, and serial number." A study by Psychologist Robert Kraut of Carnegie Mellon University suggests that the use of the Internet leads to shrinking social support and happiness. In short, one becomes alone in a crowd. Alone. Again. And NOT naturally. What is done for the sake of efficiency and proficiency can result in employees who feel adrift from any true bonding that superior teams exhibit.

COMMUNICATION TECHNOLOGY

Messages are sent via e-mail and handheld devices. Fabulous tools. Great at quick hits and few-word responses. U.C. Berkeley's School of Information Management and System Research claims that in 2002 people around the globe sent and received 400,000 terabytes of information by e-mail. That's equal to 40,000 Libraries of Congress! Forgetting the SPAM and the chain letters that say you'll have bad luck forever if you don't send them to 30 people, that's still a TON of messaging. And since we are now years from that research, you can probably multiply those terabytes exponentially.

But how many of those terabytes represent TRUE connecting? Technology can override tenderness— particularly when we're sending messages to the person just down the hall. While **E**-mail might conserve the physical energy of a face-to-face meeting, too often the **"E"** stands for ESCALATION and ERROR or ELUSIVE and EMPTY.

> *"In all the time I have been on her team, she has never ONCE stepped into my office. I just get one-sentence commands over e-mail. It is so demoralizing. I feel like I'm a programmed rat."*
>
> —Senior biochemist in a research facility

"Too Much to Do and Too Little Time"

You know this mantra. We're bristling with to-do lists and a plate filled high with expectations and expediencies, with competing demands and conflicting priorities.

> "Talk isn't cheap. It's too expensive. Can't waste a minute. If I pick up the phone, I'll have to talk to them. Or worse, I'll be stuck in a doom loop of a voice mail hell in which I will NEVER get a person."
>
> —Manager in a professional services organization

E-mail is quick. Blast off a response. Forget actual phone conversation. And heaven knows that a one-to-one meeting is way too time consuming. Oh we're so efficient—and so disconnected.

Enough with all the "reasons." No more excuses!

The heart of the matter is this: People don't follow a signature block or a global voice mail. They follow a human being who is available, articulate, and attentive to the business needs and the people around them.

Now that we've seen common excuses why we *don't* talk, let's find out how we can begin *to* talk.

START WITH THE TALK INSIDE YOUR HEAD

Every piece of communication, verbal or written, begins with a conversation in our heads. We talk to ourselves all the time, making observations, analyses, and conclusions about people, events, and actions. What employees and peers eventually hear or read is the result of that internal, infernal chatter.

Let's slow it down. There's a good possibility that you've been talking so fast to yourself that you're not even aware of the assumptions you're making or the impact you are producing. You might be shooting yourself in the foot with your mouth or that lightning-fast "send" button.

It's a blind spot. Rather like spinach on the teeth, you don't see it but other people do. Blind spots like these abound:

- You think you've communicated clearly. Instead, people are left scratching their heads.

- You think you've communicated with just the right people. Instead, there's a roster of rank and file who want to receive and give input to you.

- You think your team supports you, but you're picking up rumblings of dissatisfaction.

- Your best employee just astounded you with his letter of resignation. You had NO idea!

It's time to shine a light on potential blind spots and find out just how accurate YOUR internal assumptions are.

QUESTIONS

- Do you give rapid-fire assignments and walk away, hoping that everything was clear?

- Do you only listen to a closed circle of people and reject input from others? If you do, why?

- Who are your internal or external clients, and when was the last time you had a deep conversation with them about how you might better serve them?

- Who needs positive feedback from you, and when was the last time you gave it?

- Who needs corrective feedback from you, and how will you give it so it helps rather than hinders?

- Do you ask your employees what YOU might do to increase their levels of engagement? If not, what's stopping you?

- If you find yourself talking negatively about another employee, what assumptions are you making, and are they true? How do you know—really know—they are true?

The answers to these questions begin to identify the employees with whom open conversation would be priceless and skilled listening would be golden.

MOVE FROM NO SIGHT
TO INSIGHT

In order to uncover your personal blind spots and model great communication behavior, you must be able to:

1. Ask questions that encourage people to open up.

2. Practice naïve listening to the answers you receive.

The latter is probably more important. **Naïve listening** means to listen as if you are hearing something for the first time—even if you are not. It means to withhold judgment while the person is speaking.

"Seek first to understand rather than to be understood" is as true now as it was when St. Francis of Assisi wrote his peace prayer and when author Stephen Covey popularized it in *Seven Habits of Highly Effective People*. The practice of astute questioning followed by naïve and non-defensive listening results in understanding.

> *"The Lord gave us two ears and a mouth which should mean we're supposed to listen twice as much as we speak."*
>
> —Irish Proverb

Questions That Require Naïve/ Non-defensive Listening

- What might be something I do that gets in the way of your optimum performance?

- If you could change anything about this department, organization, process, etc., what would that be and why?

- Please tell me what you understand are the most important aspects of your work?

- What talent do you have that we have either not tapped or have not used to its full potential?

- What matters most to you about your work?

Naïve listening is done with the ears AND the body. Does the following bring forth a memory?

"Doesn't matter what I think. My manager will ask for input but then sarcastically put it down, roll his eyes, or make some dismissive gesture. Only his viewpoint matters. I have plenty of ideas, but why bother. I'm just hanging on for two more years and then I'm out of here."

—Machinery Operator of a manufacturing assembly line

So you don't fall into this trap, here's an example. I coached one leader so he'd guard the tone of his voice and the look on his face when his direct reports gave him feedback. He kept his vocal tone warm and neutral and his body language open versus closed. He was the model of "naïve listening." He nodded his head as they talked, summarized what he understood them to say, and asked for clarification and specific examples. He earned more loyalty and following by asking questions and then listening intently as if he were hearing the information for the first time. He made commitments and received commitments back from his team. For the first time, they all really talked!

Use a "Talking Stick"

So, how do you hear a wide variety of ideas and uncover views that are different from yours? Consider the "talking stick." The talking stick has been used for centuries by many American Indian tribes as a means for a just and impartial hearing, allowing all voices to be heard. When used in council circles, it designated who had the right to speak. When matters of great concern came before the council, the leading elder would hold the talking stick and begin. When he finished what he had to say, he would hold out the talking stick, and whoever wished to speak after him would take it. In this manner the stick was passed from one individual to another until all who wished to speak had done so.

The talking stick not only kept order but it also fostered mutual integrity. The holder of the stick was assured free speech, no reprisals, no humiliation, and no interruptions. But with the stick also came responsibility. The speaker was charged with speaking wisely and truthfully. If he couldn't do that, he'd be quiet or else bring dishonor to himself.**

**Carol Locust, Ph.D. Native American Research and Training Center Tucson, Arizona (Tribal affiliation: Eastern Band Cherokee)

Imagine the power a talking stick could bring to departmental meeting or corporate boardrooms. It wouldn't matter whether you passed a tree limb a coffee mug, or a ballpoint pen. What is important is the honoring of mutual integrity as well as the unstated assumption that everyone is seeking to understand a much larger perspective.

Invite your team and others to a Talking Stick meeting. Notice the word *invite*. People are free not to show up. Coercion is not an invitation. When people are invited, those who care the most show up.

> "It is essential to employ, trust, and reward those whose perspective, ability, and judgment are radically different from yours."
>
> —Dee Hock

TALKING STICK MEETING CHECKLIST

☑ Create a focus question while stating that people are to speak freely.

☑ Form a real circle. This brings equality.

☑ Use a talking stick or other object and state the guidelines: anyone may speak with no interruptions and no humiliation.

☑ Let everyone know that there are no reprisals for anything that is said. (Disregard this statement and you will have done a world of hurt to your credibility.)

☑ Only the person holding the stick can talk, and the agreement is that the words must be honest. The stick is then passed around. I've used everything from a stone to a very old teddy bear, the latter being a favorite of one of my all-male teams.

☑ When everyone has spoken who wishes to, summarize what has been said and what you will do with the information.

For most people, this will be an experience that seldom happens in corporate life. This might very well become a critical retention tool as well as a source for innovation and competitive advantage.

TURN VIEWPOINTS INTO VIEWING POINTS

A viewpoint is your singular way of seeing an issue, much like a miner's light focuses on a small vein of silver. A viewing point, however, is taking in as wide a view as possible, much like a stadium light illuminates all corners of a playing field. The wider your lens, the more connections you can make and the more encompassing your impact. This is exactly what you can achieve when you convene a Talking Stick meeting: a viewing point versus your singular viewpoint.

But it doesn't require a circle of people. It can happen on a smaller scale. Here's an example:

We moved into an old house that should have had a view of the not-too distant ocean. The problem: The house below us had allowed trees to grow thereby cutting off the view. Next-door neighbors told us that these down-the hill owners were not cooperative and would not cut the trees. They had a definite viewpoint!

I called the down-hill neighbors and invited them to come up after work for a glass of wine or a cup of tea. Said we'd like to know them better. Surprised by my call, they agreed to join us.

On the appointed day, they arrived and I ushered them to the backyard for our visit. They stopped in their tracks. "My goodness, what a view you'd have…if…" The trees were cut within the week. In all the years they had lived down the hill, no owner of our house had EVER invited them up to see just what their trees blocked. Viewpoints changed to literal viewing points.

Similarly, in a consulting assignment with an insurance company, we had the claims people ride along with sales. Sales folks came in and worked on claims. What had been an antagonistic situation turned around because each saw their counterpart's world and suddenly understood. Conversation went from hostile to helpful. They went from a viewpoint to a viewing point.

Whose mountain top do you need to experience?

SUMMARY—PRICELESS TALK:
Where do you start?

▶ Start talking and get to work.

▶ Leave behind the excuses of time, technology, and team separated by distance.

▶ Uncover your personal blind spots through astute questions and naïve listening.

▶ Make it safe (no reprisals) for people to give you feedback.

▶ Create opportunities for differing opinions by using a talking stick.

▶ Exchange viewpoints to arrive at a viewing point.

WORDS TO REMEMBER

"The leader has to be practical and a realist, yet must talk the language of the visionary and the idealist."

—Eric Hoffer

"When people talk, listen completely. Most people never listen."

—Ernest Hemingway

"Wise men talk because they have something to say; fools talk because they have to say something."

—Plato

"There is no conversation more boring than the one where everybody agrees."

—Michel de Montaigne

"The secret of success in conversation is to be able to disagree without being disagreeable."

—Anonymous

"To listen well is as powerful a means of influence as to talk well and is as essential to all true conversation."

—Chinese proverb

"You cannot truly listen to anyone and do anything else at the same time."

—M. Scott Peck

Priceless Talk:

Whom do you talk to?

ASK THE "ORANGE BATONS"

Next time you're at an airport, observe the men and women who wave orange batons over their heads to direct arriving planes into the correct gates. There's a very practical reason for their actions.

On the tarmac, in front of each gate, is a line in the shape of the letter "J." The pilot must place the front wheels of the plane on that line. But there's a problem: The pilot can't see the baseline from the cockpit. Only the orange baton holders can view the J-line. They are the literal frontline and serve as the pilot's eyes.

Who are your frontline people—your "orange batons"? Who are closer to the action, the problem, and the customer than you are? What do they know that you don't know, can't see, or don't hear?

I learned the power of talking to orange batons from Tom Kilpatrick, former head of training for USS-Posco, a steel finishing plant in Pittsburg, California. Tom told me of taking over the command of a ship in the Navy in which the commander had been removed "for cause." This ship had the highest rate of pending disciplinary actions and the lowest reenlistment rates. When Tom left the ship two years later, he had totally reversed those numbers.

"How did you do that?" I asked with amazement. "Two years!"

Tom explained that within the first three weeks of his command, he was in his bunk thinking: "What would be the most miserable place on this ship, in the middle of the night, in the summer, in the South Seas?" Answer: "The engine room!"

He got up, went to the galley, grabbed orange juice and glasses and went to the engine room. He served juice around and then asked the crew, "Tell me what I need to know to help you do a great job and want to stay in the Navy."

By morning, that story had spread like wildfire throughout the ship. Earned him more loyalty than anything else he did. It worked because of four things:

1. He showed up where he was least expected.

2. He came seeking understanding and a broader viewing point.

3. He asked a probing question and then listened—deeply.

4. He acted on what he heard, and if he couldn't act, he told them why.

Where might your presence be needed so you can "serve orange juice"? Who is in your engine room? Too often in business, managers fail to take advantage of the eyes and ears of the "front" folks. The orange batons are the ones you really need to TALK to. Ask what they see, hear, and know.

PAY ATTENTION TO "LITTLE DAVIDS"

When Patrick Harker, Dean of Wharton School, was asked what made the critical difference in the school's most successful fund-raising campaign ($425 million in six years), he replied that he made it a priority to engage the next generation of alumni leadership.

Listening to the voice of David is a tradition from the Middle Ages and the Benedictines. The abbot of a monastery made decisions after getting the input from all the monks, beginning with the youngest monk. Had the elders in the Old Testament listened to the young kid with the slingshot, the giant Goliath would have been dispatched quickly. Little David was right,

> *"Words of wisdom are spoken by children at least as often as scientists."*
>
> —James Newman, American Astronaut

but it took time for the tribe to understand that young (or new) did not mean "unskilled."

Who are the newest and/or youngest on the team—*your Davids*? It is often the newest members who ask the most discerning questions. They are not jaded by politics, the past, or protocol.

Ask them for their opinions. Tell them that you expect them to teach you something at the end of three months. I guarantee that those employees will search high and wide to bring you innovation or, at the very least, an insight into some of your procedures, products, or services.

"When you seek out junior voices, two things surprise you: how much those young alumni have to say and how important it is. At the same time, so many of them — people who have achieved extraordinary success — feel as though they're not being taken seriously. I've learned that lesson multiple times during my career, and it's about listening to what I call 'the voice of David.'"

—Patrick Harker in *Fast Company* magazine, September 2003

WALK OUT AND TALK OUT

The best conversations are face-to-face. Leaders know the power of their presence. Great leaders literally go out and seek information.

Procter & Gamble's A. G. Lafley, selected as the 2006 CEO of the Year by *Chief Executive* magazine, is known for working hard for about 90 minutes and then getting up, walking around, and chatting. This isn't just a whim. It's a core value that confirms his desire to see, hear, and touch employees as well as consumers. That's a value that has had him walking around barrios in Brazil in order to get close to the customers. And it's one of the principles that has revitalized a 169-year-old company and its employees.

Where is your presence needed? Get out and go talk. And LISTEN naïvely.

Marriott Chairman and CEO, Bill Marriott, Jr., was noted for telling his general managers that when he visited their properties, he better NOT find them at their desks. Instead, he expected them out talking and listening to employees and guests. Stay in a Marriott today and there's a good chance you'll see that face-to-face conversation in action.

"You can't stay in your corner of the forest waiting for others to come to you. You have to go to them sometimes."

—Winnie the Pooh

SUMMARY—PRICELESS TALK:
Whom do you talk to?

▶ Make a list of the people who are closest to an issue, a process, a program—your orange batons.

▶ Ask them to tell you what they see and hear.

▶ Make a list of the newest members of your team—your Little Davids.

▶ Ask them to look with "new eyes" at their jobs. What makes sense? What seems like a waste of time? What idea or innovation might they come up with?

▶ Take all of their responses seriously. If you can use them, tell them why and thank them. If you can't, tell them why.

▶ Get away from your desk, your office, and your car. Talk to people where the action is. Visit another site. Talk, ask, listen, and learn.

"Making things happen still requires the ability to make people like you, respect you, listen to you, and want to connect to you. And by connect, I mean connect personally, not digitally...The human connection will always, always, always outrank the digital connection as a get-ahead skill."

—Dr. Karl Albrecht
Author of *The Power of Minds at Work* and *Corporate Radar*

Priceless Talk:

What do you say?

REMEMBER THAT FACTS TELL
BUT EMOTION SELLS

I magine if Patrick Henry, hero in the American Revolution, stood up in a ta
ern and gave statistics about the number of taxes the British Parliament ha
imposed on the colonies. Data delivered, he would sit, waiting for the rousir
rally to action. I guarantee you, it wouldn't happen.

Nor could you imagine any kind of response if Martin Luther King, Jr., in h
most famous speech, said "I have a hunch." What King did was to describe
dream, a value, and make it all real by painting a picture that people could se
with their own eyes. People could line up behind that dream. Unfortunatel
many leaders at all different levels of organizations succumb frequently to th
blah blah of jargon and Wall Street. They provoke only yawns and no energ
Energy comes from the excitement of a picture well-painted, of living large, c
being part of something that matters deeply.

People are drawn to organizations of purpose rather than policy. And
leader who can see such destiny is the magnet that keeps great employees. It
this leader who has the courage to speak boldly and with conviction and trutl

If you've never had this type of conversation with the folks around you, it
time to start. What is bigger than the bottom line to you? To them? Why are yo
in this business? Why do THEY think you're in business? It's not just mone
Working for shareholder return was never a reason to jump out of bed. Profit is th
applause you get because you are *excited* by working for a bigger "something."

In the American culture, work answers the question "Who are you?" Th
Ritz-Carlton insists that their employees are "ladies and gentlemen servin
ladies and gentlemen." That very wording elevates everyone within the hote

When my mother was in her 70s and still working for Blue Cross/Blue Shiel
of Florida, she said that her job was to "ease the pain of the seniors." Prett
funny when you considered her age.

Mom was lucky. She had figured this out by herself. Most of us need help figuring out what would get us emotionally excited about work. One leader asks his team, "What would you like your children to say about your work?" He gets answers that can astound you.

Use this approach to define mission statements and departmental visions. You'll begin to move from providing information to creating inspiration.

Soft? Consider this mission statement that business consultant Ian Percy found and placed in his marvelous book, *Going Deep*: "*Our mission is to find meaning in our work and to help our members experience joy, satisfaction, happiness, and celebration.*" Think that came from a religious sect? Wrong! It's from one local of the International Brotherhood of Electrical Workers. And I guarantee you—it only came because they TALKED about what was emotionally important about their work. Save the dollars and stats for yearly goals. But connect through emotion.

P.S. You can't do this by e-mail. Emoticons are NOT emotions.

ADD CONTEXT TO YOUR CONTENT

If I stood in an empty room, talked out loud, waved my arms, and strode up and down, you'd say I was nuts. However, put 750 people in a room and suddenly, I am a professional speaker. It's all a matter of context.

What is the context (situation, environment, challenge) in which you find your organization, your department, or your team?

> "*Context and memory play powerful roles in all the truly great meals in one's life.*"
>
> —Anthony Bourdain

Let's say you're getting ready to announce a reorganization and a consolidation of office space. Announce that in a vacuum and people think you're arbitrary. Instead, lay out the context: a competitor has entered your market and is gobbling up market share. You want more people in face-to-face positions calling on customers and solidifying relationships. Extra office space is a redundancy that is foolish in the current setting. That context forms the backdrop for "why we are doing what we're doing."

Without context, actions can seem superfluous or ill-conceived. Talk about current realities, how people fit in, and what role they play. Context creates meaning and without meaning, people feel meaningless.

Talk to people with as much candor as possible. Don't fabricate, paint rosy pictures, pretend, or hide. Notice I said "talk," not e-mail. Employees are more likely to respond, to rise to the task, to ask questions, and to help solve the challenges once they understand the current realities.

SHARE WHAT'S BEHIND THE CURTAIN

In *The Wizard of Oz*, the little wizard created a persona that was basically a sham. He projected a larger-than-life image on a curtain that both awed and scared the folks in the Emerald City.

> "We suspect that what humans really appreciate is attention from humans, not computers."
>
> —Thomas Davenport and John Beck, *The Attention Economy*

He thought that in order to lead others, he had to be something he was not. In the end, the curtain was pulled away and we saw him manipulating a false image of himself. He said he was bad at wizardry. And he was! But he also turned out to be a wise man, using his powers of observation to help the Cowardly Lion, the Tin Man, the Scarecrow, and Dorothy discover their strengths. Had the curtain not been ripped away, no one—including the wizard—would have been able to use their true talents.

Your team needs to see and know the real you. You can't hide behind a curtain or a "persona." For people to follow you, to believe in your vision for the future, you must be willing to talk about your strengths *and* areas for improvement. If you're a smart leader, you've hired people because they possess skills and abilities that you don't. TALK about what you bring and what they bring "to the party." Such honest disclosure engages people at a deep level. It lets people SEE behind your curtain—a critical element for building trust within your team and encouraging others to pull back their curtains as well.

How do you pull back your curtain?

Try completing these sentences with your team:

- The biggest mistake I ever made was…
- The greatest lesson I've learned is…
- I need your help with…
- You can count on me to…
- What makes me crazy at work is when…
- Here's what I expect of you…
- The best way to get my attention is…

PRACTICE STORYTELLING INSTEAD OF TELLING

Go into any organization and talk to employees. Ask them what the company is like. They won't hand you an annual report or an employee manual. They tell stories that put flesh and bone on an organization's culture and practices.

> *"Storytelling is fundamental to the human search for meaning."*
>
> —Mary Catherine Bateson

Good storytelling is an important method for outlining goals, getting results, and creating culture. It lets you transmit values, calm the grapevine, and share knowledge.

Southwest Airlines doesn't have to instruct employees in how to behave. Instead, they swap stories that talk about flight attendants' antics, about the vice president of operations who delivered the mail to help out a short-staffed mail room, about the regular customer who baked cookies for the ground crew.

When I helped a surgical device manufacturer design a recruitment video, we didn't start off talking about career pathing. Instead, we told the stories of patients whose lives changed because of the work this company did.

If I wanted to make the point that customer service saves money, I wouldn't just "tell the fact." Instead, I'd create an example that told a customer's story and what it cost the company at each connection point in the business.

To jumpstart your storytelling, work on these basics:

- What story would put flesh and bone on the point you want to make?

- Inspire with phrases such as "Imagine if…" "An experience that taught me was…" "I knew this mattered when…" "John is a service hero because…"

- Ask your internal and external customers this question: "Please describe a day-in-your-life that will help me understand our product and how you use it."

Stories don't have to be long. In fact, sometimes a few sentences let people create a story of their own. When Kennedy talked about putting a man on the moon, he caught a nation's imagination. Had he talked about rocket thrust and space competition, it would have been "ho hum." He actually started a story that continued in people's imagination and moved to the airwaves.

If you think of storytelling as a business narrative that engages the mind and heart, you'll start to see that it can help the leader's challenge to spark action, develop teams, and take people into the future.

> "Man cannot live without story any more than he can live without bread."
>
> —Dr. Warren Bennis

TELL PEOPLE WHAT THEY CAN DO, NOT WHAT THEY CAN'T DO

There's something about the word "can't" that raises the hairs on our necks. Maybe we don't like limits being set for us. Maybe we are just rebellious kids at heart.

Think about it. You hear the word "can't" and immediately your internal conversations start with:

"Why not?"

"See. I knew she wouldn't listen."

"Oh yeah! Just watch me."

Regardless, all of us would do well to heed the advice of communication specialists and minimize our use of the word "can't." Tell people what you CAN do—what THEY CAN do. For example: "You can have your vacation June 19." "What I can do for you is..." "Here's what you can do..." "Tell me what you think YOU can do in this situation." Sounds like a small shift, but it is the small things in communication that make all the difference in the world.

We're so accustomed to using "can't" that this switch will require effort. It takes practice but is well worth the effort. The difference between CAN and CANNOT is shorter in letters but longer in results.

"Few things in the world are more powerful than a positive push. A smile. A word of optimism and hope. A 'you can do it' when things are tough."

—Richard M. DeVos

Improvise to Maximize

Great conversations result when there's an easy give and take, a go-with-the-flow sensation, along with an acute sense that you are being heard at a deeper level than the normal chitchat. In this instance, good conversations resemble improvisational theater.

Improv actually depends upon all the actors paying close attention to each other and then working with whatever is presented to them. Let me repeat that again: *pay attention and work with whatever is presented.*

Select someone you'd like to (or need to) talk to. Open up the conversation by stating either why you've initiated the conversation or by asking an open-ended question. Then, practice these techniques:

- **Encourage talking by saying, "Yes…tell me more."** This means that no matter what is stated, don't change the subject, get defensive, fail to listen, or ignore the response. You have the opportunity to create new and positive results by building upon whatever is said.

- **Don't plan your response** while the other person is speaking.

- **Seek what is provocative, interesting, or new** in what you are hearing. There's a gift somewhere. Trust me. Ask the other person to expand on something that intrigues you—even if it bothers you.

- **Work with what is given.** In the 2004 presidential debates, rarely did either candidate "work with" what the other said. Instead, each hauled out a party line that left the viewer less than excited about either candidate. A smart leader can take a question in a meeting—even a question that sounds antagonistic—and work with it. Example: One manager challenged another in a meeting by saying, "Your people need to be more visible to senior management!" The response was something like this: "That's interesting. What does visible look like to you?" The ensuing conversation was both instructive and powerful, leaving the "challenger" looking petty and clueless.

DON'T JUST SAY SOMETHING...
STAND THERE...
AND THINK

Too many of us shoot from the lip. We see or hear something and instantly have a retort or a comment when we truly haven't gotten all the facts. The more emotionally hooked we are, the more likely we are to get into knee-jerk mode.

The more critical the relationship or the event, the more critical it is to take a deep breath and think before you speak, or as my dad use to say, "Put your brain in gear before your mouth is in action." It's hard to improvise if you have tapped into the fight-or-flight response. Stop. Hush. Think.

I've seen leaders who deliver "parking lot memos." They hear something in the parking lot and by the time they get to their desk, they've formulated an e-mail and sent it off to the supposed offender. Unfortunately, they didn't get all the facts. When investigating an issue, watch out for the phrase "Why did you?" It automatically assumes guilt. Instead, ask, "What happened?" This garners more information and puts your brain in the driver's seat.

Perhaps we think a leader has to have an immediate response because we value speed. Think of some of the comments leaders in both the public and private sector have made that are off-the-cuff remarks which come out as everything from senseless to clueless.

The wrong talk can carry a stiff penalty. If you are emotionally hooked–hush up, think, and THEN talk. This takes tremendous personal awareness and maturity. SO—know you'll blow it at times. Just learn and go on.

*"I don't talk about the differences,
because what I'm trying to create is a
shared vision. I try to instigate conversation
about what the company's values
look like as images."*

—Grace McGartland, *Thunderbolt Thinking*

SUMMARY—Priceless Talk:
What do you say?

▶ Get people engaged through emotional connections rather than just facts.

▶ Use stories to make vivid points.

▶ Give people the context for your words. What's happening NOW that allows your team to make sense of your words and actions?

▶ Share what's behind the curtain: your talents and deficits.

▶ Reframe messages to tell people what "can" happen versus what "can't."

▶ Work with what is given.

▶ When emotionally hooked, hush up, think, then talk.

MORE WORDS TO REMEMBER

"In the absence of information, people will connect the dots in the most pathological way possible."

—Leslie Charles

"The single biggest problem in communication is the illusion that it has taken place."

—George Bernard Shaw

"The opposite of talking isn't waiting to speak. The opposite of talking is being open to hear."

—Eileen McDargh

"If you have an important point to make, don't try to be subtle or clever. Use a pile driver."

—Winston Churchill

"If you can't explain an idea or a policy plainly in one or two sentences, it's not yours; and if it's not yours, no one you speak to will be persuaded of it...or...know what you are."

—Stanley Fish

Priceless Talk:

How will they feel?

USE SCRIPTING FOR CORRECTIVE CONVERSATIONS

I've never met anyone who actually enjoyed giving performance reviews or holding difficult conversations. In many cases, we'd rather drop hints, write a note, or wait until we're so mad, we explode.

That's not fair to you or your employee. And it also sends a mixed message to the rest of your team.

Scripting is a marvelous tool for being assertive without being aggressive. Like a literal script, you write it out in advance so you are prepared. It's a great talking tool for executives, team leaders, and everyone in between.

When **scripting a corrective conversation**, plan how you will:

DESCRIBE	the situation, the event, or the issue. Use terms that are specific, here and now, and without generalizations. Don't dig up a history of past offenses.
EXPRESS	your feelings about this issue and/or how it impacts others.
SPECIFY	what you want the person to do (or to stop doing).
EXPLAIN	the consequences that will occur if the situation does (or does not) change.

Here's an example: "Susan, you've been late six times in the last two weeks. When that happens, the phones aren't covered, your team is scrambling to help our clients, and I am frankly very annoyed and concerned. This is not like you, and I depend upon your presence. I need you to tell me what's going on and what you will do to fix this. As a consequence I'll feel better and the team will feel more supported."

You've just laid out the case as you see it. You have opened the door for vital talk. All manner of things might come up. You might discover that she's been experiencing nocturnal migraines and is sick in the morning. You might discover that the daycare center has closed, and she has to take the baby to a center that is much farther away. You might discover that there are some tensions in the department, and this is an escape mechanism. Or you may discover that she has been just plain negligent.

Regardless of what the person says—at least (by scripting) you will have addressed the issue in a non-emotional, business-like manner. And you'll increase the odds of getting the results you want.

TREAT GRATITUDE AS A GIFT

A captain of industry was once heard saying that a pat on the back is only a short distance from a kick in the pants but goes a heck of a lot further in getting results. But gratitude is deeper than an "atta boy" or the term "thank you." Besides, how many times has someone tossed out a casual "thanks" and you thought, "Ummph. If only they KNEW how much I did"?

> *"God gave you a gift of 86,400 seconds today. Have you used one to say 'thank you'?"*
>
> —William Arthur Ward

Dr. Ken Blanchard taught me the **elements of effective praise** back in the days when I lectured on his behalf across Canada:

- Specifically state what was done.

- Express how you feel about it and what it means to you or the company.

- State what skill, attitude, whatever it took for the act to occur.

- Say *thank you.*

Here's an example of all the elements together:

> *"Joel, yesterday you took a great deal of your time to carefully go over my manuscript and to point out what worked, what didn't, and why. I felt that you actually cared not only for the results, but also for me as a writer. It took courage to tell me some things as well as generosity to tell me what was good. I'm really delighted to be working with someone like you. Thanks!"*

Remember, a great thank-you allows people to know that you truly observed what they did. By identifying the behavior, you up the chances they can replicate it. And it also says that you sincerely valued what they did.

If you must use e-mail, try the same format, but elect e-mail only as the last resort. E-mail has become so commonplace, so haphazard, and so impersonal, that it can really lose its impact.

> *"I'll send your assistant, Trudy, a bouquet of roses and you send her a bouquet of emoticons. Let me know what she likes best."*
>
> —Brian Collins, Former Creative Director, Ogilvy & Mather in a debate with Kevin Roberts, Worldwide CEO Saatchi & Saatchi

Of course, there's nothing wrong with chocolate and wine. And the greatest thank-you is the gift of time. Not a gold watch but time away from the office.

BE UNCOMMON

Common courtesy isn't common. Be uncommon. In an age of rude answers, coarse language, and flippant remarks, we've lost the *please*, the *pardon me*, the *no problem*, and the use of a person's name. We've forgotten to shut off the cell phone during a conversation with another person, or to guard what we say out loud where other people can hear. We forget that a smile can be heard over a phone and that it's just plain rude to tap our messages on our handheld during a meeting.

Because it is rare, courteous conversation can be a unique competitive advantage in getting and keeping employees as well as customers.

"Courtesy is the one coin you can never have too much of or be stingy with."

—John Wanamaker, American merchant and founder
of one of the first American department stores

See how you fare on this simple courtesy quiz:

1. I always say *please* and *thank you*—regardless of age or rank.

2. I never interrupt others.

3. I am respectful of others' beliefs.

4. I call people by their appropriate name.

5. I refrain from side comments and snide remarks in a meeting.

6. I look at people when I talk to them.

HELP WITH HUMOR

Talk can also be funny. Not the sarcastic biting humor of put-downs and inside jokes, but rather the humor that can lighten a difficult situation or put something in perspective.

A travel agency was known for helping its agents get through difficult customers by awarding the Order of the SALMON. At the end of the week, agents would know which agent had the most challenging week with customers yet still managed to keep a positive interaction going. With much fanfare, the agent explained the challenge and was urged to exaggerate and use as much humor as possible. She was then awarded a plastic salmon for her ability to SWIM UP STREAM.

> *"Laughter is the shortest distance between two people."*
>
> —Victor Borge

Being able to talk about the week, laugh at the difficulties, and be rewarded for staying calm helped generate both fun and connection within the office.

Laughter can put people at ease if it is used to acknowledge what everyone is thinking. I was asked to speak at a convention in which the main session room temperature hovered around 50 degrees. People were wrapped in tablecloths. By the end of the second day, it still had not warmed up. When it was my turn to talk, I welcomed them by saying, "Welcome to the land of the frozen chosen."

Gales of laughter and applause burst out. And it made a point. The attendees were CHOSEN to be there. It was a privilege.

"If I can get you to laugh with me, you like me better,

which makes you more open to my ideas.

And if I can persuade you to laugh at the

particular point I make, by laughing at it,

you acknowledge its truth."

—John Cleese, of
Monty Python fame

SUMMARY—PRICELESS TALK:
How will they feel?

▶ Use scripting in advance of any corrective conversation.

▶ Learn how to give praise in a four-step process that encourages similar behavior.

▶ Practice courtesy with everyone.

▶ Lighten up. People feel better when they laugh.

Priceless Talk:

Why does it matter?

WATCH YOUR WORDS

Words are tools to tame, teach, or terrorize others. And some of the most complex words are in the English language. Where else but in English does *economy* mean small in a car and large in a tube of toothpaste? Where else but in English does *fair* run the gamut from two stars on the movie rating scale to a gorgeous day? Now add to this verbal soup our multicultural environment and employees for whom English is a second language. For a bit of spice, throw in all the acronyms that mean "nothing to nobody" except the initiated, and you have a true tower of babble, blubber, and bewilderment.

Talk is priceless when you stop and clarify just what terms mean to people. Example: One of my hospital clients was creating a very complicated (and time consuming) piece of software to allow nurses to input treatment plans and patient progress. After agonizing for months, they discovered that simple words meant different things to a rehab nurse, a case manager, and a physical therapist. The project ended in a mess.

Accents can also turn words into everything from humorous to dangerous. One manager, born in the Deep South, was upset because an employee did not deliver a package on time to a warehouse. The employee insisted that she couldn't find the location. What finally came to light was that the manager's Southern accent turned warehouse into WIREhouse. No wonder the employee couldn't find it.

> *"The difference between the right word and the wrong word is the difference between lightning and lightning bug."*
>
> —Mark Twain

HERE'S HOW TO HANDLE THE CHALLENGES WITH WORDS:

- Ask people to clarify critical terms. For example, when we say *customers*, exactly to whom are we referring? If you say, "I need it soon," exactly what does *soon* mean?

- Never assume that relatively new employees understand all the acronyms if you are in an acronym-heavy business. When I heard someone say, "The head of the MCB is concerned about our FMOT," I stood speechless. So too did the employees who had been there less than two months. (MCB=Market Centered Business and FMOT=First Moment of Truth.) Say what??

- Ask people to paraphrase what you said so that you can make sure you communicated clearly. And if what you hear back is not what you intended, YOU own the error. Not the hearer.

- Beware of generalizations like *never* and *always*. Rarely are we accurate when we use such adverbs.

MAKE IT SAFE TO ADMIT MISTAKES

Part of authentic conversation is owning up to the fact that one isn't perfect. An honest apology or an admittance of error speaks volumes to the courage of a leader and can add to credibility. Make the "Law of No Reprisals" a given for everyone in your sphere of influence. Hiding bad news or mistakes leads to nasty surprises.

My colleague, Dr. Terry Paulson, tells of a manager who placed $100 on a table and proceeded to tell his assembled team of a mistake he made and what it would cost the company. He then looked around the room and announced that the money would go to any employee who could top his mistake. (Ummm—trust issue here, yes? Remember the Law of No Reprisals.)

Turned out, someone did top the manager's mistake. The manager handed out the $100 bill and concluded, "That's the best training money I ever spent. Why should we risk repeating mistakes when we can learn from others?"

> *"A leader is one who knows the way, goes the way, and shows the way."*
>
> —John C. Maxwell

One CEO of a large travel firm was given feedback that he was a lousy listener. He cut people off, finished their sentences, rarely looked people in the eye, and generally only gave lip service to honest give-and-take-conversation. Not only did he publicly apologize to his employees, but he signed up for a class on listening. (Yes—this is a skill that is taught!) He then asked employees to help him practice the lessons.

Wow. What a powerful move. Personal power is always more attractive and engaging than positional power. You are perceived as being personally powerful when you do those things that require courage or authenticity. Admitting mistakes and offering apologies require both.

GO AWAY SO YOU CAN GET CLOSER

Take a retreat to advance. Bring your team to a location that is away from work. Ban cell phones and handheld devices until after your gathering.

"Every now and then go away...for when you come back to your work your judgment will be surer."

—Leonardo da Vinci

Instead, talk with each other. Talk formally with the help of a facilitator. Use assessments to understand communication styles and behaviors. Share insights. Ask how to develop stronger relationships. Identify what gets in the way.

Then—tackle the issues. Use the talking stick. Make decisions. Listen to each other. Define terms. Talk informally, over a meal, over a walk, over an after-hours cup of coffee. I've seen amazing results when I've helped teams talk to each other. The creation of a cohesive unit begins with conversation. Sometimes you just need a catalyst.

BUILD RAPPORT WITH YOUR PRESENCE

Tom Rath, head of research and leadership development at the Gallup Organization, says "When people have a close relationship with their boss, it doubles the chances of them being engaged on the job and being more productive."

As a leader, your physical presence or your voice over a phone is the best way to develop relationships with employees and colleagues. It is all about rapport. We establish rapport with people in two primary ways: visual and vocal. The visual is the most powerful. It involves things like eye contact, body postures which mirror the other person, and even placement at a table. (Side-by-side sends a collabo rative signal. Sitting across the table can set up adversarial signals.)

Vocal, the second strongest rapport builder, refers to the "music your voice makes." Allow your voice to pick up the rhythm and pace of whomever you are talking to. If they have a more rapid pace, increase yours. If their voice is soft er, moderate yours.

PAY ATTENTION AND PRACTICE.
IT WILL TAKE TIME.

"The average American now has just two close friends. One in four people say they have no close friends. Sociologists say we are becoming more isolated because of suburban migration, long work hours, and the growing amount of time spent on the internet, iPods, and other electronic devices."

—USA Today

SUMMARY—PRICELESS TALK:
Why does it matter?

▶ Seek clarification and expanded meaning. Words don't mean the same thing to everyone.

▶ Watch out for acronyms and make sure all understand this internal form of shorthand.

▶ Celebrate people who admit to making mistakes.

▶ Take your team away to talk, tackle issues, and improve team cohesiveness.

▶ Create rapport by using your voice and physical presence to "mirror" the other person.

Talking—it seems so ordinary—so every day—so easy. Maybe that's why we take this skill so for granted. Truth is—if it were easy—we wouldn't have so many disconnected work teams around us. We wouldn't hear that the number one complaint in organizational life is poor communication. With the technology temptations, talking has become a rare and priceless commodity. Who would ever guess that a competitive advantage would be to have a LIVE human answer a telephone!

Remember, the "softest skills" in leadership are the hardest skills in leadership. Hopefully, you're now convinced that talk is indeed the ticket for better connections and better connections lead to greater success…for everyone.

You've just read a number of ways to improve your communication. Work on one thing at a time. Your effort to make more authentic, personal connections will speak volumes in and of itself. Your employees might wonder what got into you. Just smile and say, "I've been talking to myself about talking to others. And I've been listening."

The choice is now yours. The ball is in your court. The table has been set. It's your turn.

Now go find someone to talk to.

About the Author

Eileen McDargh, CSP, CPAE

Since beginning her consulting and training practice in 1980, Eileen has become noted for her ability to speak the truth with clarity, wisdom, humor, and compassion. Long-standing clients and repeat engagements attest to her commitment to make a difference in minds, hearts, and spirits of organizations and individuals. For successive years, *Executive Excellence* magazine has ranked her as one of the top 100 thought leaders in business leadership.

She draws upon practical business know-how, life experiences, and years of consulting to major national and international organizations that have ranged from global pharmaceuticals to the US Armed Forces, from health care associations to religious institutions, from American Airlines to Xerox, from 3M to IBM, from drill foremen in the Arctic to brokers on Wall Street.

She authored *Work for a Living & Still Be Free to Live,* the first book on work/life balance—a topic that placed her as a futurist in this issue and continues to be published in revised editions. Eileen's other books include *Gifts from the Mountain: Simple Truth for Life's Complexities* and *The Resilient Spirit: Staying Rightside Up in an Upside Down World*. She is a featured author in *A Woman's Way to Incredible Success,* and a contributing author in *Meditations for the Road Warrior.* Her three-part video training program, *Engaging the Spirit of Nurse Leadership,* is in constant demand within the health care arena.

She served as one of ten faculty members in a business television series, *Reclaiming Business Excellence,* and has headlined with speakers like NBA coach Pat Riley, Notre Dame's former coach Lou Holtz, Dr. Ken Blanchard, executive strategist Marshall Goldsmith, William Bridges, and boardroom poet David Whyte.

Eileen is a certified speaking professional (CSP), and her election into the CPAE Speaker Hall of Fame places her among the top 3% of the 4500-member National Speakers Association.

Contact her at *www.eileenmcdargh.com* or (949) 496-8640.

About The Publisher

Since 1977, WalkTheTalk.com has helped organizations and individuals, world wide, achieve success through Ethical Leadership and Values-Based Business Practices. And we're ready to do the same for you!

We offer a full-range of proven resources and customized services – all designed to help you turn shared values like Integrity, Respect, Responsibility, Customer Service, Trust and Commitment into workplace realities.

To learn more about WalkTheTalk.com or order additional copies of this high-impact handbook, call 888.822.9255 or visit walkthetalk.com.

WALKTHETALK.COM

Resources for Personal and Professional Success

Discover our full range of products and services to include:

▶ "How To" Handbooks and Support Material

▶ Video Training Programs

▶ Inspirational Gift Books and Movies

▶ Do-It-Yourself Training Resources

▶ Motivational Newsletter

▶ The popular *Santa's Leadership Secrets* and *Start Right...Stay Right* product lines

▶ 360° Feedback Processes

▶ and much more!

Other Books by WalkTheTalk.com

Start Right…Stay Right
Every employee's straight-talk guide to personal responsibility and job success. Focusing on attitudes and behaviors, this best-seller is a "must read" for seasoned employees as well as new staff additions. $9.95

The Manager's Communication Handbook
This cut-to-the-chase resource provides leaders with simple, easy-to-follow guidelines for positively affecting employee performance. $9.95

Five Star Teamwork
Within these pages, you'll find a collection of ideas, strategies, tips, and techniques to help make your teams the best they can be – ones that deliver the business results you want and need. $9.95

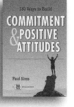

180 Ways to Build Commitment and Positive Attitudes
This NEW Walk The Talk handbook provides individuals and leaders with practical tools to turn attitudes into effective actions in a way that builds commitment to desired results. $9.95

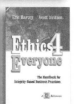

180 Ways to Walk the Customer Service Talk
Packed with powerful strategies and tips to cultivate world-class customer service, this handbook promises to be the answer to getting everyone "Walking The Customer Service Talk" and building a reputation of service integrity. $9.95

Ethics4Everyone
This unique and powerful resource provides practical information to guide individual actions, decisions and daily behaviors. When it comes to ethics, everyone is responsible ... everything counts! $9.95

ORDER FORM

Have questions? Need assistance? Call 1.888.822.9255

 Please send me additional copies of TALK AIN'T CHEAP...IT'S PRICELESS

1-24 copies: $10.95 ea.   25-99 copies: $9.95 ea.   100-499 copies: $8.95 ea.   500+ copies: *Please call*

TALK AIN'T CHEAP...IT'S PRICELESS _____copies   X $_____   = $_____

Additional Resources

Start Right...Stay Right	_____copies	X	$	9.95	= $	_____
Managers Communication Handbook	_____copies	X	$	9.95	= $	_____
Five Star Teamwork	_____copies	X	$	9.95	= $	_____
180 Ways — Attitudes	_____copies	X	$	9.95	= $	_____
180 Ways — Customer Service	_____copies	X	$	9.95	= $	_____
Ethics4Everyone	_____copies	X	$	9.95	= $	_____

Product Total $_____

*Shipping & Handling $_____

Subtotal $_____

Sales Tax:

TX Sales Tax – 8.25% $_____

(Sales & Use Tax Collected on TX & CA Customers Only)

CA Sales/Use Tax $_____

TOTAL (U.S. Dollars Only) $_____

*Shipping and Handling Charges

No. of Items	1-4	5-9	10-24	25-49	50-99	100-199	200+
Total Shipping	$6.75	$10.95	$17.95	$26.95	$48.95	$84.95	$89.95+$0.25/book

Call 972.899.8300 for quote if outside continental U.S. Orders are shipped ground delivery 3-5 business days.
Next and 2nd business day delivery available – call 1.888.822.9255.

Name_____   Title _____

Organization _____

Shipping Address _____
_{No P.O. Boxes}

City_____ State_____ Zip _____

Phone _____ Fax _____

E-Mail _____

Charge Your Order: ❑ MasterCard   ❑ Visa   ❑ American Express

Credit Card Number_____ Exp._____

❑ Check Enclosed (Payable to: The WALK THE TALK Company)

❑ Please Invoice (Orders over $250 ONLY) P.O. # (required) _____

Prices effective June, 2007 are subject to change.

PHONE 1.888.822.9255 *or* 972.899.8300 M-F, 8:30 – 5:00 Central	**FAX** 972.899.9291 **ONLINE** www.WalkTheTalk.com	**MAIL** WALK THE TALK CO. 1100 Parker Square, Suite 250 Flower Mound, TX 75028